RHAPSODY

BY CAROLYN MILLER

ISBN 978-1-5400-4001-5

WILLIS MUSIC

EXCLUSIVELY DISTRIBUTED BY

HAL•LEONARD®

Visit Hal Leonard Online at
www.halleonard.com

Contact us:
Hal Leonard
7777 West Bluemound Road
Milwaukee, WI 53213
Email: info@halleonard.com

In Europe, contact:
Hal Leonard Europe Limited
42 Wigmore Street
Marylebone, London, W1U 2RN
Email: info@halleonardeurope.com

In Australia, contact:
Hal Leonard Australia Pty. Ltd.
4 Lentara Court
Cheltenham, Victoria, 3192 Australia
Email: info@halleonard.com.au

PREFACE

The idea for this book began when an invitation arrived from the Hattiesburg Music Teachers League to be their guest composer for their Composer Festival in 2019. The festival, held every two years, features the music of a guest composer. It also commissions a brand new solo for the event. I was asked to compose a new piece at the late intermediate level, and that solo is "Rhapsody in D Minor."

You know the ending to this story: I enjoyed composing at the mid to late intermediate level so much that I began composing more pieces at this level, and it soon became an entire collection. You will find a wide variety of styles including one solo with a gentle swing, another featuring adventuring knights, as well as two dramatic rhapsodies.

I hope you enjoy playing them as much as I enjoyed writing them.

Carolyn Miller

CONTENTS

Performance Notes

Knights of Spain

This piece continues the adventures of the "knights" (they first appear in my *Lyrical Style* books). It begins with a chord trumpet fanfare. Notice that the fifth finger holds down the melody, even though the pedal changes at the beginning of measures 8–10. Measure 12 introduces a modal melody, like a faraway guitar. Be sure to play deeply into the keys here. Measures 20–26 should be easy to play—but only if you've practiced your arpeggios! End with a *grandioso* feel: the knights have reached the end of their journey.

Lazy Day

This fun, relaxed piece is to be played with a swing feel. Take your time and let the stress-free mood come across. Measure 32 might look intimidating, but look closely: these are simply inversions of the same diminished chord. Personally, I enjoy playing measure 25 to the end.

Swirling Traffic

As you play this piece, visualize what morning traffic usually looks like, especially in a big city. Everyone is in a hurry. Drivers are impatient because traffic is slow. There is a short relief section in measures 17–19, before the traffic picks up again. At the end, create the image of a successful arrival to your destination.

Sunset

Imagine a beautiful sunset at the beach. This solo should create a calm mood as you play the expressive melody with gentle waves of *crescendo* and *decrescendo*.

Rhapsody in D Minor

This piece requires deep *forte* chords and good finger dexterity. The melody enters with the right hand in measure 9 after a theatrical beginning. The continuous 16th-note pattern played by the left hand requires steadiness, and must have gentle waves of *crescendo* and *diminuendo*. At measure 29, the key changes to D Major for a brief respite. Showcase the *cantabile* countermelody here as much as you can. At measure 45, the original minor key returns and should lead to an exciting, dramatic conclusion.

Stormy Seas

Composed in 2012, "Stormy Seas" should sound exactly as its title describes: tumbling arpeggios blown about by strong winds! My editor decided to add this piece to the collection because its mood matched several of those in this book. There is a lull in the storm at measure 25, but it doesn't last for long. Build to an electrifying end.

P.S. If you want to hear an example of what this piece should sound like, there is an existing video of me playing this piece on YouTube!

Rhapsody Mystique

After a short introduction, a mystical melody begins. It returns several times, and each time must be played with a singing tone and with much feeling. The piece moves through several different moods, so try to bring out each one. Near the end (measures 63–66), carefully observe the chord patterns. This will make the dramatic *forte* ending easier to play.

Knights in Spain

Carolyn Miller

Majestic ♩ = c. 82

The knights escort the Royal Family to Spain

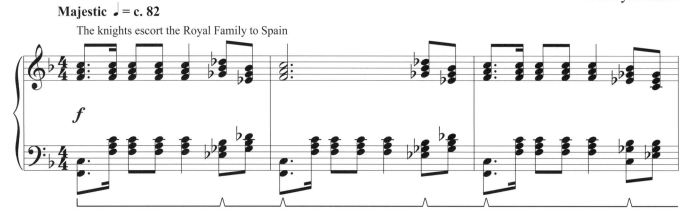

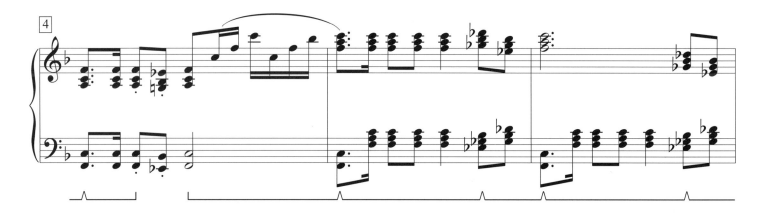

They pass a little town, and hear a faraway guitar

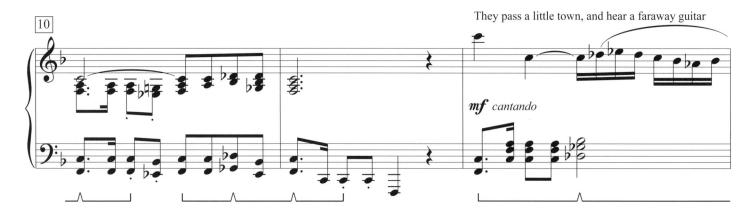

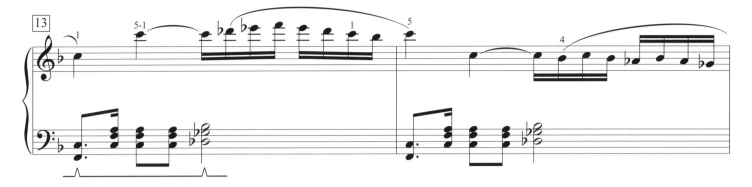

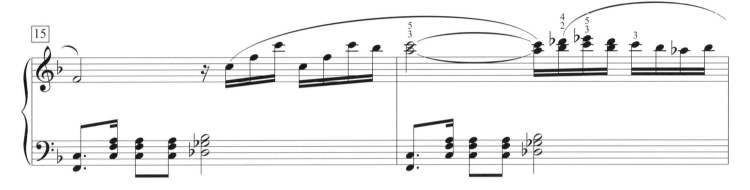

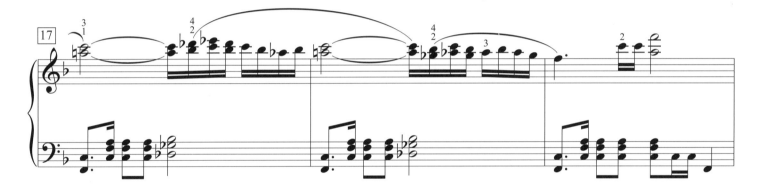

Crowds greet and cheer

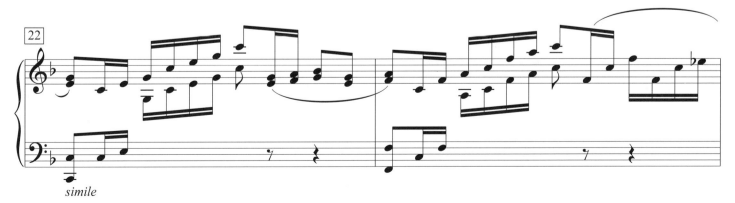

simile

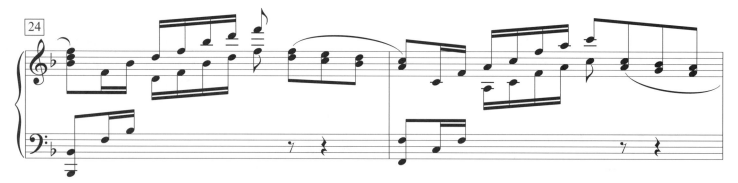

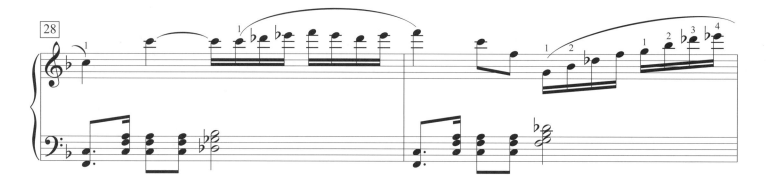

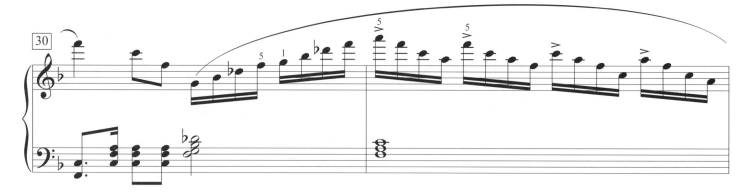

They have arrived!

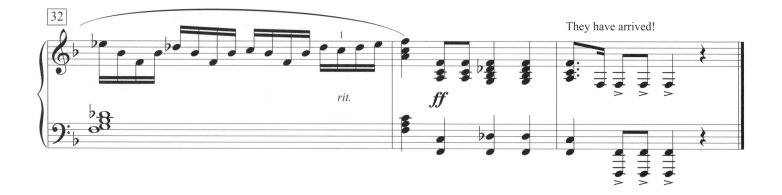

Lazy Day

Carolyn Miller

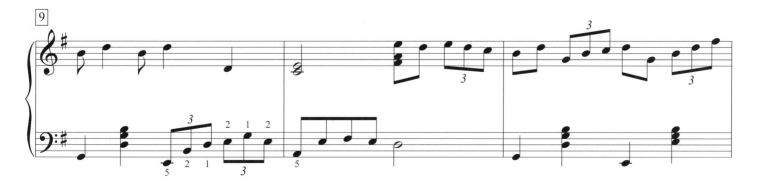

Swirling Traffic

Carolyn Miller

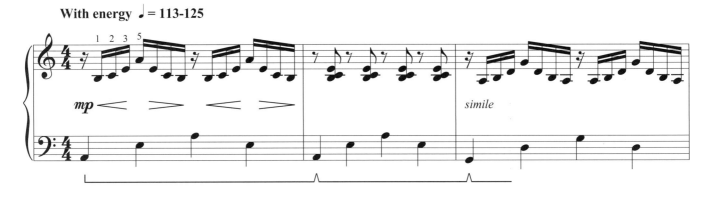

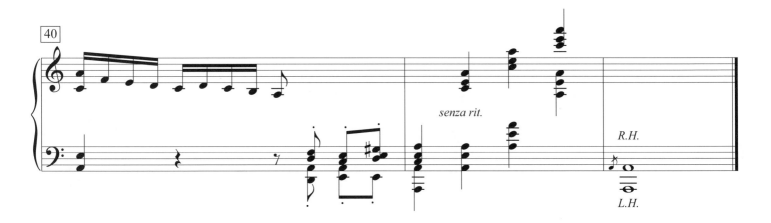

Sunset

Carolyn Miller

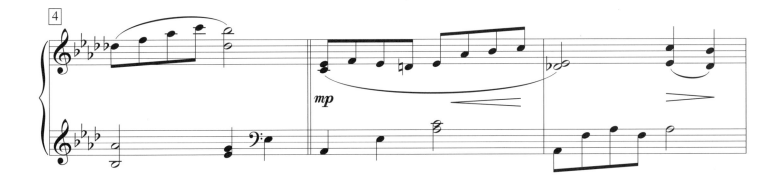

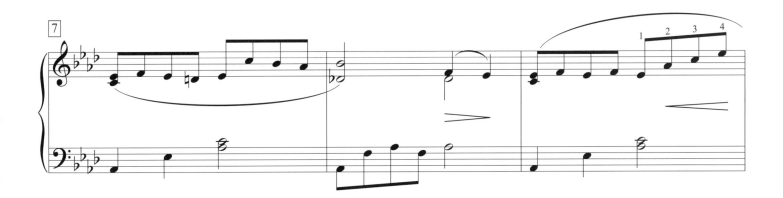

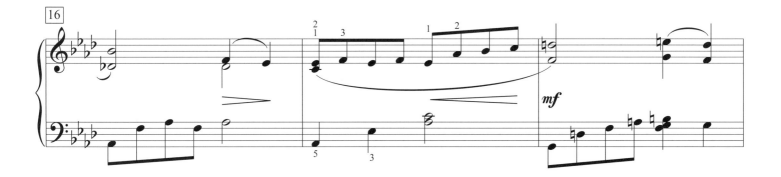

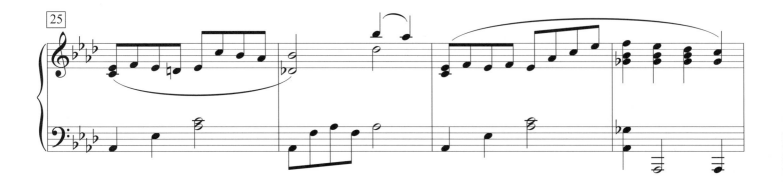

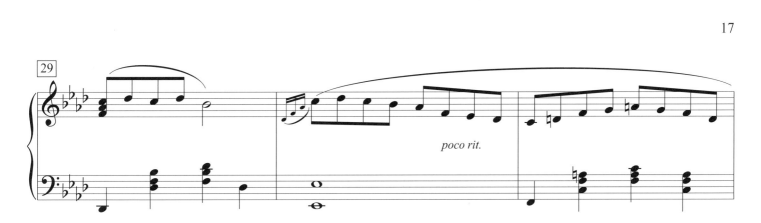

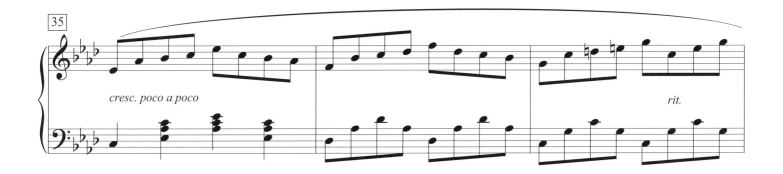

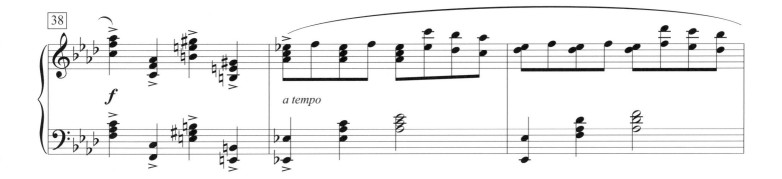

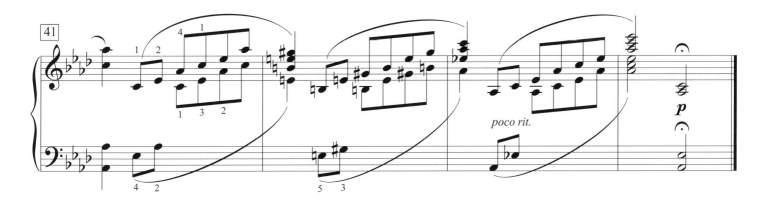

Rhapsody in D Minor

Dedicated to the Hattiesburg Music Teachers League of Hattiesburg, Mississippi,
in honor of their 2019 Composer Festival

Carolyn Miller

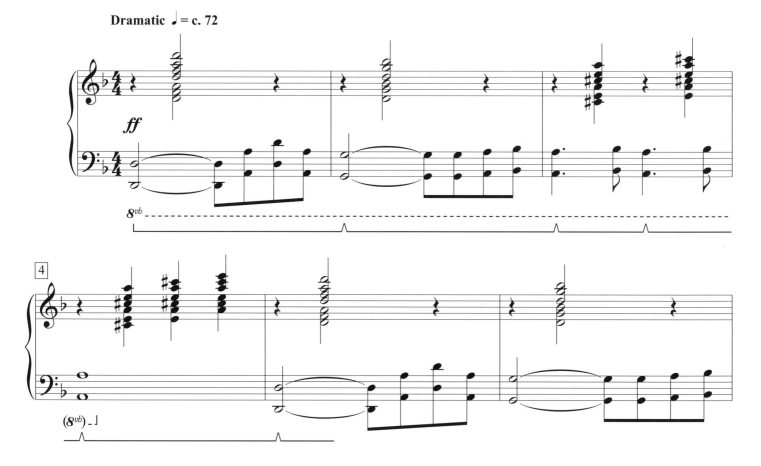

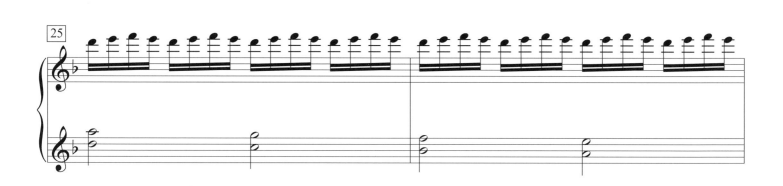

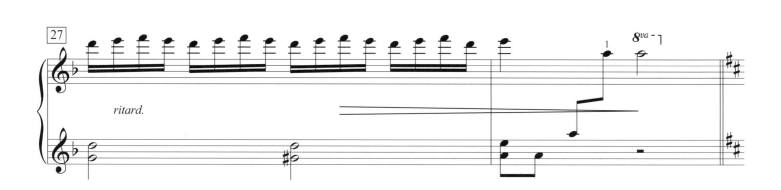

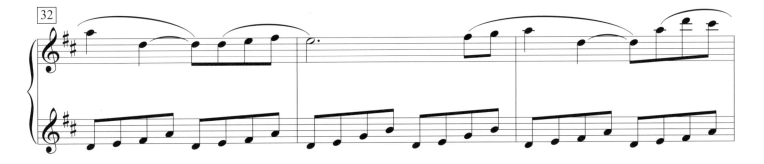

Tempo Primo

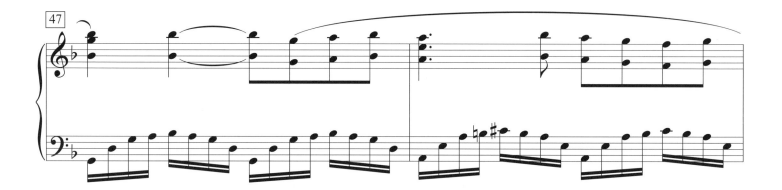

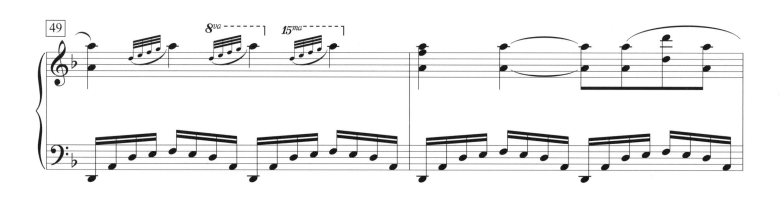

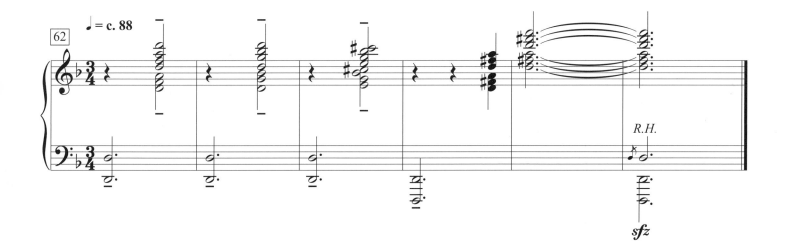

Stormy Seas

Carolyn Miller

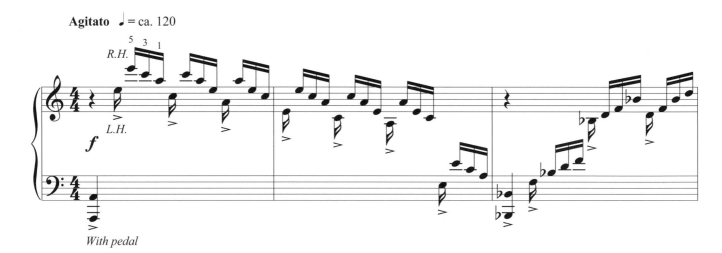

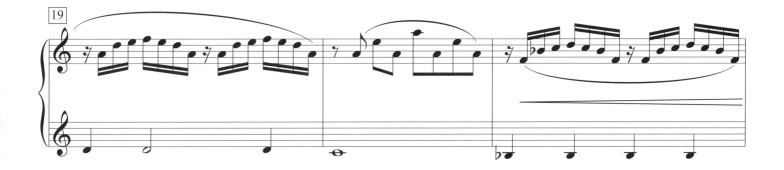

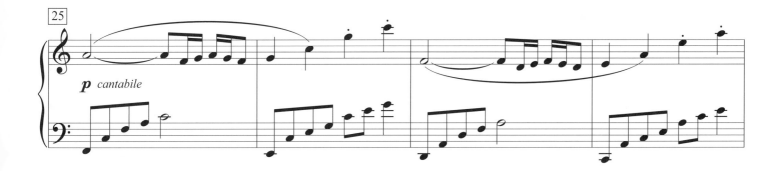

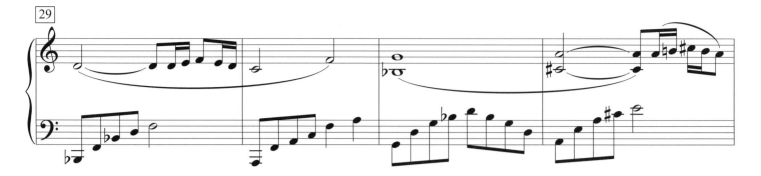

D.C. al Coda

CODA

Rhapsody Mystique

for Kathleen Jendrusik

Carolyn Miller

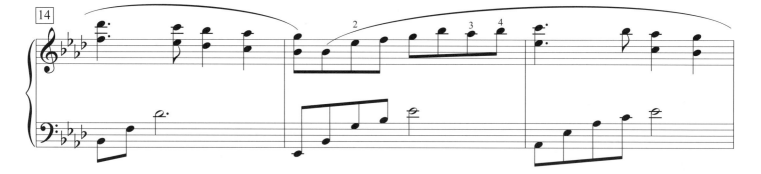

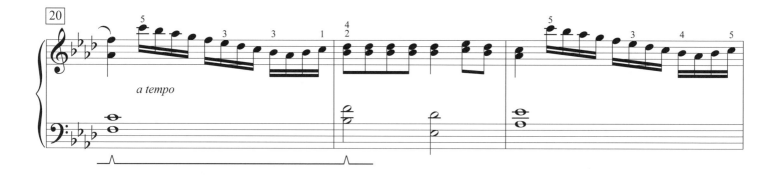

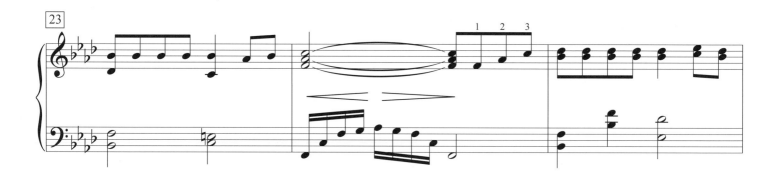

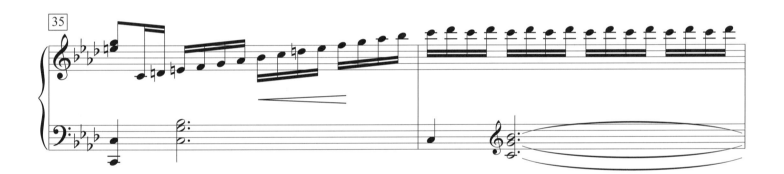

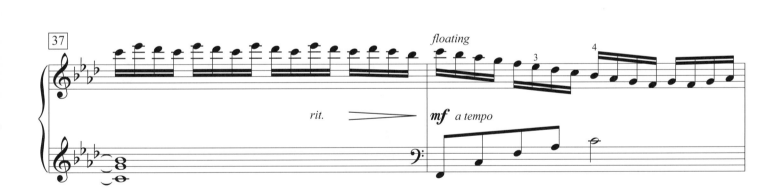

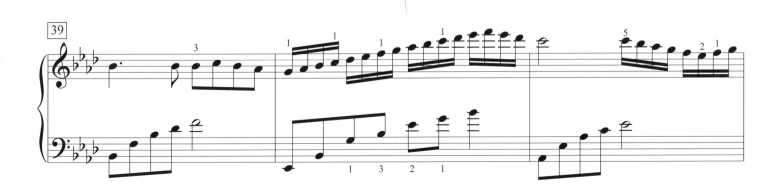

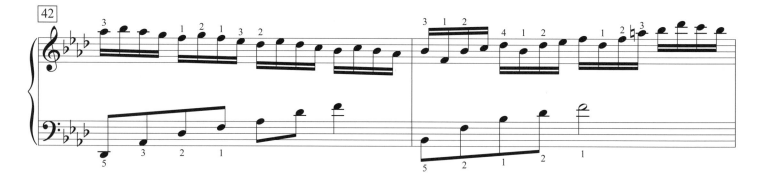

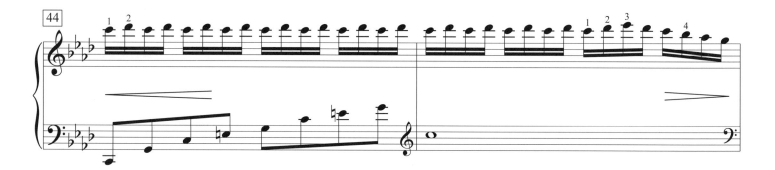

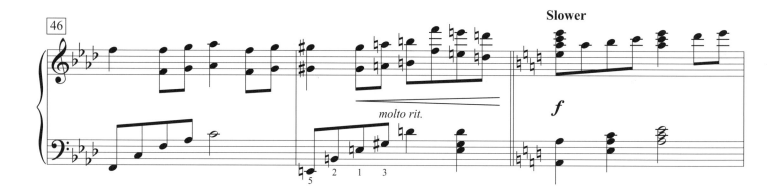

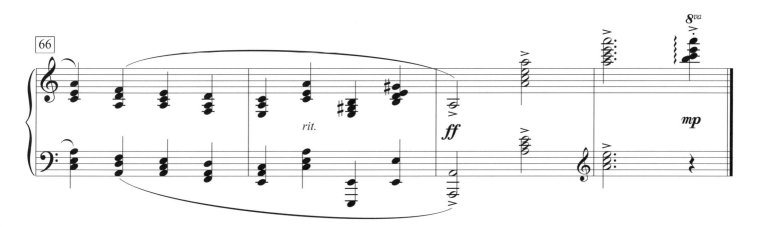

ALSO BY CAROLYN MILLER

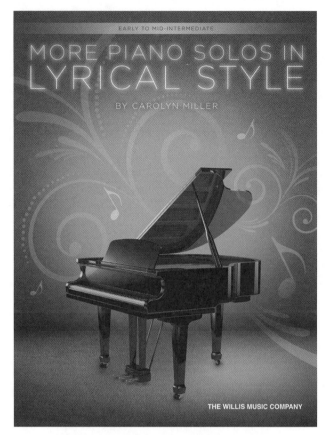

PIANO SOLOS IN LYRICAL STYLE
HL00124389

Titles: Dancing in the Rain • Falling Snowflakes
Island Breeze • Knights of the Castle
Longing • Remembrance • Tango Español

MORE PIANO SOLOS IN LYRICAL STYLE
HL00243885

Titles: Deep Thoughts • Dizzy Fingers
Knights of the Kingdom • Little Tango
Matter of Fact • Meditation in G
Simplicity • Storybook Waltz

Carolyn Miller's popular *Piano Solos in Lyrical Style* books
feature wonderful recital solos for the expressive young student.
The pieces progress from early to mid-intermediate.